The Ancient Egyptian City of Thebes: The History and Legacy of the Capital that Became Luxor

By Charles River Editors

The Temple of Seti

About Charles River Editors

Charles River Editors provides superior editing and original writing services across the digital publishing industry, with the expertise to create digital content for publishers across a vast range of subject matter. In addition to providing original digital content for third party publishers, we also republish civilization's greatest literary works, bringing them to new generations of readers via ebooks.

Sign up here to receive updates about free books as we publish them, and visit Our Kindle Author Page to browse today's free promotions and our most recently published Kindle titles.

Introduction

A mural on the burial chamber of Nefertari, wife of Ramses II

Thebes

"Let [Agamemnon] offer me the wealth…of Egyptian Thebes, the richest city in the whole world…which has a hundred gates through each of which two hundred may drive at once with their chariots and horses…but not even so shall he move me." – Homer, *The Iliad*

Africa may have given rise to the first humans, and Egypt probably gave rise to the first great civilizations, which continue to fascinate modern societies across the globe nearly 5,000 years later. From the Library and Lighthouse of Alexandria to the Great Pyramid at Giza, the Ancient Egyptians produced several wonders of the world, revolutionized architecture and construction, created some of the world's first systems of mathematics and medicine, and established language and art that spread across the known world. With world-famous leaders like King Tut and

Cleopatra, it's no wonder that today's world has so many Egyptologists.

In just a few lines of his renowned *Iliad*, Homer immortalized in writing what the Thebans had immortalized in stone nearly a millennium before - Thebes "of the Hundred Gates" was home to some of the most splendid relics of the religion, history, and art of ancient Egypt and indeed of all the ancient world. As Thebes grew from an unimportant settlement to the richest city in the ancient world, unparalleled in its beauty and splendor, nearly all of its leaders left his or her mark in the form of one or more legendary monuments at the great temple complex to Amun-Ra at Karnak, the temple to Amun-Ra at Luxor, and the mortuary temples and tombs of the Valley of the Kings. As Thebes underwent the dramatic changes that came with its 3,000 years of political shifts, religious reforms, and ritual changes - not to mention its sometimes abrupt changes in fortune - its monuments grew and changed with it. The study of the fascinating archaeology of these sprawling structures thus provides an excellent point of entry for understanding nearly all aspects of Theban history and culture.

The Ancient Egyptian City of Thebes: The History and Legacy of the Capital that Became Luxor examines the history of the city and examines the architecture of the ancient Egyptian capital. Along with pictures of important people, places, and events, you will learn about Thebes like never before, in no time at all.

The Ancient Egyptian City of Thebes: The History and Legacy of the Capital that Became Luxor
About Charles River Editors
Introduction
   Chapter 1: Early History
   Chapter 2: The New Kingdom Period
   Chapter 3: The Amarna Period
   Chapter 4: The New Kingdom Period
   Chapter 5: The Intermediate Period and Late Period
   Chapter 6: The Ptolemies and Beyond
   Online Resources
   Bibliography

Chapter 1: Early History

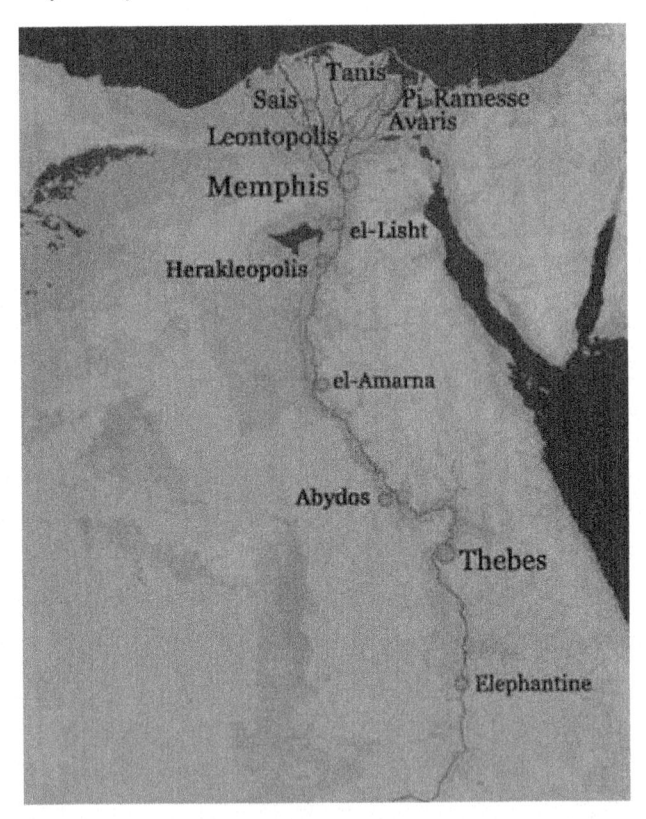

A map of Ancient Egypt

Like all such magnificent projects, the great monuments of Thebes were not built in a day; in fact, the settlement of Thebes predates the construction of its major monuments by at least a millennium. Archaeologists at el-Tarif, a site located on the west bank of the Nile at Thebes, have unearthed stone artifacts, pottery, and parts of buildings, all of which indicates that Thebes was settled at some point during the late Neolithic period from 3700-3300 BCE. The finds at el-Tarif are relatively meager, and while archaeologists suspect that there were larger areas of settlement now buried beneath the alluvium of the Nile, they have found no evidence that early Thebes was of any more or less importance than its neighboring settlements.

By the end of the third millennium, Egypt, under the government of the Old Kingdom pharaohs

(2686-2181 BCE), had achieved its first continuous peak of civilization. However, despite some evidence of royal building activity at Thebes during this period (a small temple to Amun may have been constructed at Karnak during the Old Kingdom period), Thebes was still nothing more than a relatively unimportant settlement. That said, any settlement which was not at Memphis, the capital of the empire at the time, was relatively unimportant during the Old Kingdom period; nearly all the wealth of the Egyptian Empire went to glorifying the pharaohs of the third, fourth, and fifth dynasties at Memphis, and to the construction of their extravagant tombs in the legendary pyramids on the opposite side of the Nile at Giza, Saqqara, Dashur, and Meidum. Since the pyramid industry demanded nearly all the materials and labor available within the empire, significant local building projects were all but impossible.

The beginning of the Theban ascent to prosperity is contemporaneous with the collapse of the Old Kingdom government and its pyramid industry at Memphis. At the end of the 21st century BCE, three successive Theban warlords (Inyotef I, Inyotef II, and Inyotef III) took advantage of the growing Egyptian power vacuum by styling themselves as pharaohs. Although the rule of Inyotef III did not extend north of Abydos, their descendant Mentuhotep I (2060-2010 BCE) was soon able to reunite the divided empire, a feat which singlehandedly started Egypt's Middle Kingdom period. Later Egyptians not only considered Mentuhotep I to be one of the greatest pharaohs of Ancient Egypt, they also saw him as one of the great founders of the Egyptian nation.

Picture of a king list at Karnak that has part of Mentuhotep I's name on it

Picture of the ruins of a sitting statue of Mentuhotep I

Like his forefathers, Mentuhotep I ruled from Thebes, and under his lengthy rule, a number of important building projects were accomplished at sites around Thebes, including Abydos, Deir el-Bahri, el-Kab, Tod, Gebelein, and Dendera. Of these great structures, only Mentuhotep's mortuary temple and tomb, found within the embayment of the cliffs at Deir el-Bahr, have survived.

Mentuhotep I was the first pharaoh to build at Deit el-Bahri. He may have been inspired by the resemblance of al-Qurn (the highest point in the Theban hills) to the pyramids of the Old Kingdom, but whatever the case, his tomb consisted of the basic elements of an Old Kingdom pyramid complex. However, Mentuhotep I arranged these elements in a highly innovative way. A causeway led from a valley temple into his tomb's large forecourt, and off to the right lay the entrance way to an unfinished burial chamber, in which was found a painted statue of the king. A portico with a double colonnade whose reliefs depicted boat processions, military campaigns, and hunting scenes was located at the rear of the tomb's forecourt.

From this portico, a ramp led up through a grove of sycamores and tamarisks to the top of a terrace. The terrace was a broad, T-shaped platform whose stem extended back into the cliff side. At the building's rear were six cubical shrines, and behind each of these was a vertical shaft of considerable depth that led to a burial chamber. These six shrines and tombs may have belonged to six royal ladies who had predeceased the king.

Beyond the outer building stood a cloistered court, which contained the entrance to Mentuhotep's actual tomb. The court led into a hypostyle hall[1] which boasted 80 octagonal columns, an altar, and a deep niche, which was presumably for a statue. Mentuhotep I's actual tomb was accessed through a passageway in the cloistered court that led deep beneath the cliff into a granite-lined burial chamber, which contained an alabaster and granite shrine in which the king's mummy was believed to have been stored.

After the death of the great Mentuhotep I, Amenemhat I (1991-1962 BCE), the first pharaoh of the 12th dynasty, interrupted the growing prosperity at Thebes by moving the Egyptian capital from Thebes to Itj-tawy, a site north of the Fayuum at el-Lisht. As the court and its workers moved away to the new capital, Thebes fell into decline, but Amun, the patron god of Thebes, had by this point become quite popular, so Thebes remained a major religious center. The cult of Amun remained important to the later pharaohs of the 12th dynasty, and they continued to lavish their attention upon his cult, especially by building him great monuments at Thebes.

---

[1] A great hallway whose main entrance was used for processions. Its side doors were used for more regular offerings of food and drink to the gods. The interior of a hypostyle hall was entirely filled with columns so that the distance between columns was less than the thickness of each column. These columns were believed to support the heavens, though they sometimes also represented the marshes that surrounded the mythological Mound of Creation.

A relief from Amenemhat I's mortuary complex

Though Amenemhat's successor, Senusret I (1971-1926 B.C.E.), ruled from Itj-tawy, he was nevertheless responsible for most of the construction that took place at Thebes during the Middle Kingdom period. At Karnak, a temple complex within Thebes, he built the site's earliest recognizable temple and processional kiosk, which he enclosed with a mud wall. The limestone temple to Amun probably replaced a smaller sandstone temple on the same location.

Senusret I also constructed a jubilee shrine[2] (known as the white chapel) at Karnak. This white chapel featured a small limestone bark[3] shrine which contained four interior pillars, and the shrine was surrounded by a peristyle of 12 pillars. The walls of the white chapel were decorated with raised reliefs which showed Senusret I at his jubilee festival, while sunken relief scenes on the eastern and western sides of the chapel's bases depicted various personifications of the Nile and other Egyptian lakes. Meanwhile, inscriptions on the northern and southern bases offered a record of the Ancient Egyptian *nomes* (administrative districts) and their measurements. The chapel must have been brightly painted, because traces of yellow paint can still be seen on the chapel's cornices and traces of red, white, and blue paint may be found on its columns and hieroglyphs. Senusret I's white chapel may have functioned as a festival kiosk since it featured a double throne on which the pharaoh could sit, and holes placed in each of the chapel's central columns suggest that banners were hung around the throne in order to conceal the pharaoh from the eyes of the public. Alternately, the throne may have sat statues of the pharaoh rather than the pharaoh himself.

---

[2] A shrine integral to the celebration of the *heb sed* festival—a festival that aimed to renew the reigning pharaoh's power, which was believed to invariably diminish over time. Unless somehow rectified, this depletion of power was believed to endanger the continued existence of the state. The *heb sed* festival replaced a more ancient ritual which entailed killing a king who was no long able to reign efficiently due to his increasing age. The heb sed ritual represented the symbolic burial of the old pharaoh. Once "buried," the pharaoh was coroneted for the second time, so that he might continue his rule as a new pharaoh.

[3] The "bark" was a great river barge—the most visible of the god's cult objects and a symbol of his power. The god's portable shrine, inside which his statue went forth in procession, was modeled upon the great bark. Both were the recipients of regal wealth.

An ancient bust of Senusret I

An aerial photograph of the temple complex at Karnak

Senusret I was both the first and last Middle Kingdom pharaoh to build substantively at Karnak. Though his successor, Amenemhat II, made several donations to Amun's temples, he did not construct any monuments of his own, and his descendants also eschewed building projects, preferring to focus on a number of successful military campaigns in emulation of their warlord ancestors.

The Middle Kingdom period began to wind down with the death of Amenemhat III in 1797 BCE, and the 12th dynasty ended just over a decade later when Queen Sobekneferu (1806-1802 BCE) completed her brief reign. A 13th dynasty continued to rule Egypt from el-Lisht, but they left little record of their accomplishments, most likely because turmoil ensued following the end of the 13th dynasty; many pharaohs of the many subsequent dynasties ruled from several different parts of the country, and many of their claims to rule seem to have even overlapped. In the two centuries following the end of the Middle Kingdom period, there are records of no less than 175 pharaohs belonging to five different dynasties. This tumultuous period (1782-1570) thus came to be known as Egypt's Second Intermediate Period.

Chapter 2: The New Kingdom Period

By the beginning of the 16th century, Egypt once again found itself with two competing sources of power. Ruling from the Delta as Egypt's 15th dynasty were a line of foreigners from Western Asia called the Hykos, while a native 17th dynasty controlled Upper Egypt from Thebes. By the 1570s, the two dynasties had begun to come into direct conflict with one another. The Theban pharaoh, Senqenre Tao, died in battle against the Hykos. Senqere Tao's first son, Kamose, ruled briefly in Upper Egypt, but it was the second son of Senqenre Tao, Ahmose I, who was able to capture Avaris, the Hykos' capital, and expel the Hykos from Egypt, driving them back into their Palestinian homeland. Egypt, united once again, thus reached another turning point in its history, and with Ahmose I's victory over the Hykos, the period known as the New Kingdom had begun. Though Ahmose I was the second son of a 17th dynasty pharaoh, his own achievements were so great that scholars recognize him as the founder of Egypt's 18th dynasty.

A fragment of a statue of Ahmose I

The mummified skull of Ahmose I

Ahmose was too busy warding off the Hykos from the borders of Egypt to have much time to think about the construction of monuments, but his son and successor, Amenhotep I (1526-1506), eagerly committed himself to the restoration and expansion of the Great Temple to Amun-Ra at Karnak.[4] The first pharaohs of the 18th dynasty were great warriors who led their massive armies in regular campaigns up the Nile into Nubia and across Mount Sinai into the Levant, and when they returned, they brought with them vast amounts of tribute and booty. Since the gods were owed a share of this wealth, Amenhotep I ensured that they received it in the form

---

[4] After the Theban victory in the rebellion against the Hykos, Amun acquired national importance. His newfound prominence was expressed in his fusion with the sun god, Ra; henceforth, Amun came to be known as Amun-Ra.

of renovations and expansions to their temple.

A relief of Amenhotep I found at Karnak

Although Amenhotep I left the Senusret I's Middle Kingdom temple at Karnak largely untouched, he made great changes to its surrounding area. Amenhotep I had two short walls appended to the original temple's western façade, thereby limiting access to the aisles by which the temple was flanked; he also destroyed the middle and eastern sections of the original enclosure wall, adding instead a limestone enclosure and a series of rectangular chapels which opened onto the temple's forecourt. On the temple's western edge, Amenhotep I constructed a gated limestone wall bisected with another stone wall which was lined with a series of 16 small limestone chapels (eight along each side). The northern line of chapels contained cult statues of Amun-Ra.

In the central area of Amenhotep I's new court stood the pharaoh's calcite bark temple, the walls of which contain the oldest surviving depictions of the sacred bark of the statues of the god Amun-Ra. The chapel's other relief scenes show the king's jubilee and other cultic rituals. Nine meter long screen walls flanked the northern and southern sides of the chapel, and on the chapel's short ends were wooden doors that could be closed in order to protect the sanctity of the god. Amenhotep also constructed a second chapel, a near-exact replica of the "white chapel" built by Senusret I in both size and design.

As if his projects at Karnak weren't enough of a legacy, Amenhotep was the first pharaoh to build his mortuary temple separate from his tomb. Though neither have been located, Amenhotep was worshipped by the tomb workers at Deir el-Medina as the founder and patron of their community, a fact which suggests that he was also the first pharaoh buried in the Valley of the Kings.[5]

Thutmose I (1506-1493 B.C.E), son and successor of Amenhotep I, rivaled his father when it came to extensive construction of monuments at Karnak. For his part, Thutmose I added two pylons[6], a hypostyle hall, and a pair of obelisks. The first of Thutmose's two pylons, pylon IV, served as the main entrance to the temple precinct through the middle of the 18th dynasty period. Thutmose also ordered rectangular niches built into the east face of the pylon's stonework, which were meant to contain small Osiride statues of himself. A sandstone enclosure wall connected to this pylon encircled the early 18th dynasty temple and replaced its earlier mud brick enclosure wall.

---

[5] Tomb plundering was a constant problem in Ancient Egypt. The pharaohs of the New Kingdom, fearing for their increasingly rich burials, took to concealing their tombs in an uninhabited valley in the western hills behind Dayr al-Bahri. These tombs tended to consist of a descending corridor which was interrupted by pillared chambers and vestibules, as well as by deep shafts to throw off would-be tomb robbers. At the far end of the corridor was the burial chamber which contained a stone sarcophagus in which the royal mummy was laid. Surrounding the burial chamber were a series of smaller chambers which held the furniture and other equipment the pharaoh would need in the next world. These tombs were often decorated with scenes of the dead king interacting with the deities of the underworld and illustrated renderings of magical texts similar to those found in Egyptian funerary papyri. The ceilings of many burial chambers were decorated with astronomical figures.

[6] A pylon was a pair of large rectangular towers with slightly sloping faces. These flanked a central, much lower gateway; on festival days, the god would emerge from this gateway through a set of double doors. The pylon's form signified the rising sun—its hieroglyph can be read as the hieroglyph for "horizon."

Picture of the ruins of pylon IV

Pylon IV also formed the west side of Thutmose's Wadjet Hall, a rectangular structure which, according to Ramesside inscriptions, was used for both the pharaoh's coronation ceremony and for the celebration of the jubilee festival. Wadjet Hall was constructed in two phases. The first phase saw the construction of the aforementioned rectangular niches on the eastern wall of pylon IV, and during the second phase, a second group of larger Osiride states were built to line the wall between these niches. The large statues were richly colored (some still show traces of black and blue paint), and all of the statues were enthroned; the statues on the northern side of the hall wore the double crown, while those on the hall's southern side wore the white crown.[7] Each of the hall's four sides contained fluted sandstone columns inscribed with the deeds of the pharaoh. These columns formed a covered peristyle, which protected the exposed statuary, but aside from its peristyle, Wadjet Hall was not roofed.

On the other side of Wadjet Hall, Thutmose I constructed another pylon, pylon V. Like pylon IV, pylon V and its court were connected to the new stone enclosure wall that now surrounded

---

[7] The statues existed in different forms to show homage to the union of the god Osiris with the solar god.

the temple. This pylon also contained rectangular niches in its eastern façade, and these too held small Osiride statutes of Thutmose I. As with pylon IV, larger sandstone statues of Thutmose I were placed between each niche. The court of pylon V also contained 16 fluted sandstone columns, which created a covered portico on the court's northern, western, and southern sides.

As a further contribution to the temple, Thutmose I erected a pair of obelisks[8] before the temple's main western gate. These obelisks, the first set constructed at Karnak, stood a staggering 60 feet high, and, according to their inscriptions, they were capped with brilliant pyramidions encased in aluminum. A vertical line of text inscribed on the southern obelisk reads: "made [the structure] as a monument for his father Amun-Re, foremost of the Two Lands, erecting for him two large obelisks at the double gate of the temple…" The two obelisks were believed to ensure the presence of the god within the temple.

---

[8] The obelisk was a very ancient and characteristically Egyptian monument. Originally, an obelisk was an amorphous stones set upright to represent the *benben* (mound) on which the rays of the rising sun first fell at the dawn of creation. Later obelisks—still carved from a single block of stone—were long, tapered, four-sided shafts with a pointed pyramidion at the top.

An obelisk in the temple complex from the reign of Thutmose I

Though Thutmose I had a son, Thutmose II (reigned 1493-1479), who also added a pylon, festival court, and another pair of obelisks to the front of the temple, it was his granddaughter, Queen Hatshepsut (reigned 1473-1458), the first female pharaoh, who was the real successor to the building legacy of Thutmose I at Karnak. Like her father and grandfather before her, Hatshepsut added her own pylon, pylon VIII, to the great temple. Hatshepsut's pylon was erected along the southern processional route, where it served as the southern entrance to the temple. Along its southern face stood statues of Thutmose II, Amenhotep I with his queen Ahmose-Nefertari, and Amenhotep II.

An ancient statue of Queen Hathsepsut

Queen Hathsepsut was not afraid to make major renovations to the temple's existing structure. Once she had relocated the calcite bark shrine of Amenhotep I to another part of the temple, Hatshepsut constructed a new central sanctuary (known as the palace of Ma'at) in its place. Hatshepsut also seems to have dismantled a portico of Osiris statues from the Middle Kingdom temple of Senusret I so that she could connect her new sanctuary to the ancient cult center.

Picture of the ruins of the palace of Ma'at

The palace of Ma'at was a rectangular structure comprised of a large central hall and a series of small rooms. The central room, which was covered with brightly painted relief scenes of Hatshepsut and her son, Thutmose III, protected Hatshepsut's own bark shrine, as well as the bark shrines of her successors, Thutmose III and Philip Arrhidaeus. The palace's smaller rooms seem to have offered storage for cult equipment.

Wadjet Hall was next on Hatshepsut's list of renovations. Here, the queen erected wooden papyri-form pillars and a wooden roof. Most notably, Hatshepsut raised a monumental pair of rose granite obelisks within the hypostyle hall, and inscriptions on these obelisks attest to the celebration of Hatshepsut's jubilee festival in the 16th year of her reign. These obelisks are also decorated with images of the queen (as a male pharaoh) giving offerings to the gods. Queen Hatshepsut seems to have been quite fond of obelisks, as she also ensured that the obelisks that Thutmose II had commissioned for his festival hall before he died made it to their intended destination. Hatshepsut even commissioned her own set of obelisks at the temple's eastern entrance, and ancient texts claim that these obelisks were completely covered in gold.

During the 17th and final year of her reign, Hatshepsut added a unique two room chapel - known as the "red chapel" due to the color of its stone - to the center of her newly-constructed palace. This red quartzite bark temple, located in the temple sanctuary, consisted of a vestibule and a sanctuary. It was raised on a grey diorite platform and could be accessed by short ramps on either side. Moreover, beautiful reliefs decorated the exterior sides of the red chapel. One scene shows the raising of Hatshepsut's obelisks in the Wadjet Hall, while another depicts the festival processions of the Opet and the Beautiful Feast of the Valley. The chapel's low base was adorned with a decorative kheker frieze, as well as the images of several kneeling Nile gods and other female figures. The decoration of the chapel was still unfinished upon the Queen's death in 1458.

Hatshepsut's co-ruler, nephew, stepson, and successor, Thutmose III, was eager to establish his legacy both in Egyptian governmental affairs and in monument construction at Karnak. The two elements of this goal were complementary, as Thutmose III, emulating his warrior ancestors, led his own armies into western Asia no less than 17 times in 20 years. Through these military campaigns, Thutmose III was able to considerably expand the boundaries of the Egyptian empire; in so doing, he won Egypt an immense amount of tribute and spoils. Most of this new wealth was channeled directly into lavishly renovating, expanding, and adding to the works of his ancestors at Karnak. Thutmose added a new pylon, pylon VI, between the court of pylon V and Hatshepsut's palace of Ma'at. This sixth pylon formed a new entranceway to the temple; accordingly, it featured a granite gate which was covered in electrum and decorated with reliefs of Thutmose III adoring Amun-Ra. A portico of 12 closed papyrus-form columns created the portico which lined the pylon's court. Amenhotep's limestone chapels originally stood at this court's northern and southern edges, but Thutmose III replaced these with new sandstone chapels that held votive statues of the pharaoh. The chapels' interior relief scenes featured both Thutmose II and a now-deified Amenhotep I.

A statue of Thutmose III

Just north of Hatshepsut's eighth pylon, Thutmose added a second new pylon, pylon VII, which marked the beginning of the temple's southern processional route. A colossal statue of

Thutmose III guarded each side of the pylon's doorway, and just south of these statues were two rose granite obelisks with inscriptions indicating that Thutmose III erected them to celebrate his jubilee festival and honor the god Amun-Ra. Another pair of obelisks placed between the obelisks of Thutmose I and Thutmose II in the Thutmose II festival hall bore the same inscription.

A relief on pylon VII of Thutmose III killing an enemy

In addition to those works, the most impressive of the many building projects Thutmose III undertook at Karnak was his addition of a large, rectangular temple to the eastern part of the precinct, outside of the original early 18th dynasty temple complex. A main door in the southwest corner of the new temple offered entrance to the temple complex, as did a smaller door in the middle of the building's western wall. Off the southwestern entrance was a series of nine small chambers (to the south) and a short vestibule (to the north). North of the entrance corridor lay a small room known as the "hall of ancestors," which had a list of Egypt's 61 kings (the earliest of whom ruled in the 4th dynasty) presented in the form of seated statues. Akhmenu's entrance corridor opened into a pillared hall, the roof of which was painted blue and displayed a breathtaking array of yellow stars. Supporting this magnificent roof were two rows of unique columns which were shaped like the poles of a portable tent.

To the north of the main hall stood three chapels which were decorated with relief scenes of various cult rituals and processions, including the *wehem-ankh* (procession of royal statues). A quartzite triad of Thutmose III with the gods Amun and Mut stood inside the largest of these shrines. The southeast section of the Akh-menu, which consisted of a suite of rooms that led out into a hall of 8 fluted columns, was dedicated to the god Sokar. Another block of rooms located just north of the Sokar suite was dedicated both to the pharaoh and to the ithyphallic form of the god Amun-Ra.[9]

    Most captivating of all the rooms in the Akh-menu was the legendary botanical garden of Thutmose III. This room, located in the temple's northeastern section, served as a catalog of all the exotic flora and fauna that the pharaoh had seen during his many military campaigns. While he was traveling, Thutmose III had collected specimens of rare species and lush plants that could not be found at home in Egypt, and upon his return, Thutmose III commissioned some of the best artists in the Egyptian empire to engrave the walls of his botanical room with reliefs that showed in splendid detail some of the most beautiful scenes that he had encountered during his triumphant Asian campaigns. The botanical room was further (and fittingly) adorned by four papyrus columns. From the botanical room, one could access Akh-menu's main sanctuary. Each wall within the sanctuary was lined with eight niches; each of these niches originally contained a statue of the Theban Ennad. A larger niche for the placement of the *naos*[10] was found in the rear of the sanctuary. The roof of the Akh-menu, accessed from a stairway in the northeast corner of the pillared hall, boasted a second sanctuary—a solar sanctuary, in which there stood a Heliopolitan-type solar altar, shaped like a series of *hetep*[11] symbols. In order to accommodate the Akh-menu and other enlargements to the temple structure, Thutmose III destroyed the temple's pre-existing mud brick enclosure wall and replaced it with a new wall made of sandstone.

---

[9] Amun's ithyphallic form most likely originated from the legendary conception that Aum was the "first formed" of the pantheon—since he had no father, he had to impregnate his own mother. He was therefore regarded as a god with great sexual attributes.
[10] The naos was a small, often portable shrine.
[11] "hetep" was an Egyptian symbol that represented a state of satisfaction and peace.

Jon Bodsworth's picture of columns in the Akh-menu

Though the Akh-menu was the most monumental of Thutmose III's contributions to Karnak, the pharaoh also completed a number of other, smaller, building projects at the great temple to Amun-Ra. Thutmose III oversaw the construction of a long corridor which led from Wadjet Hall and the court of the fifth pylon to the southwest entrance door of the Akh-menu temple. Lining this corridor on its south side was a series of rooms and one chapel, known as the "station of the king." The function of these rooms is unknown. East of the Akh-menu, between the eastern obelisks of Hatshepsut, Thutmose III constructed a contra temple[12] that opened to the east. This temple's façade had low screen walls, which were interspersed with six square pillars fronted by Osiride statues. On the other three sides of these pillars were decorations depicting the pharaoh as he embraced Amun-Ra. The temple's wide front hall led to a series of smaller chambers which were decorated with reliefs of the pharaoh standing before the offering tables of Amun and Min. In the temple's central chamber was a *naos* carved from a single piece of calcite, and this *naos* was home to a dyad of Thutmose III and Amun-Ra. It was in this contra temple, often called "the chapel of the hearing ear," that the Theban populace could petition (a statue of) the pharaoh as he stood with Amun-Ra.

The last of Thutmose III's many major contributions to the Great Temple at Karnak was the addition of a new sacred lake. This new lake was located to the south of the Middle Kingdom court and may have replaced an earlier sacred lake that was located somewhere in the temple's southern area. The sacred lake had multiple functions. During religious festivals, it was used for the flotillas of sacred barks, and it was enjoyed by Amun's geese.[13] Here Thutmose III also built himself a shrine (the "chapel of the lake") on a small podium that was surrounded by a peristyle of 18 columns. The chapel opened up onto the western banks of this sacred lake and onto the court of the seventh pylon. This shrine was a replica of the calcite chapel of Amenhotep I that had long ago served as the central bark shrine at Karnak. The chapel of the lake served as a convenient way-station for the portable bark of the god whenever the sacred bark came forth from the temple on a festival day to sail the sacred lake.

---

[12] A temple appended to the rear wall of a temple structure for those not allowed to enter the temple proper. Contra temples provided such individuals with a place to interact with the divinities.

[13] The goose was sacred to Amun. In one creation myth, the celestial goose ("the great cackler") laid an egg on the original mound of creation. Out of this egg hatched the sun-god, Amun-Ra.

A picture of the sacred lake

Given the amount of energy Thutmose III devoted to the expansion of Karnak, his son and successor, Amenhotep II (1427-1401 B.C.E.), chose to focus his efforts on the enlargement of smaller temples all over Egypt. Still, Amenhotep II did not entirely neglect the temple complex at Karnak. Along the southern processional route, Amenhotep II constructed a low grand festival court which seems to have held at least four separate structures, including a small pylon, a porch, and a series of pillared peristyles. Like so many of his predecessors, Amenhotep II also constructed a small calcite shrine for himself, which may have been situated between the easternmost pair of obelisks in the festival hall of Thutmose III.

Thutmose IV, the son of Amenhotep II, inherited his father's tepid attitude towards building at Karnak. The only significant contribution Thutmose IV made to the great temple was to adorn the great festival court of Thutmose II with a double peristyle of square pillars. Thutmose IV also completed a few superficial renovations to the great festival court of Thutmose II. After re-facing the walls of the hall with sandstone, Amenhotep II redecorated them with scenes of cattle being sacrificed to the gods and the pharaoh making offerings to Amun-Ra. The southern wall depicts the king, accompanied by his mother Tiaa, stretching the cord for the building. These reliefs were vividly painted in shades of red, yellow, green-blue, and blue.

Thutmose IV's peristyle at Karnak

Thutmose IV also oversaw the placement of the largest obelisk ever raised at Karnak. This obelisk, (called "the unique obelisk," stood east of the core Amun-Ra temple in the area reserved for the worship of the solar gods. The unique obelisk had originally been commissioned by Thutmose III, but the pharaoh died before the monolith could be erected.

As the Egyptian empire reached the height of its prosperity, Amenhotep III (1391-1353) was eager to construct his own legacy at Thebes. Accordingly, Amenhotep III commissioned an entirely new temple (known today as the temple of Luxor) to Amun, Mut, and Khonsu. The Temple of Luxor originally consisted of a large peristyle court, which was surrounded on three sides by a double row of papyrus-cluster columns. Beyond this forecourt lay a complex of halls and chambers. Amenhotep III was also responsible for constructing the most striking feature of the Luxor temple: a majestic colonnade of 14 columns with capitals shaped like open lotus flowers.

Pictures of the ruins of the Temple of Luxor

As if this new temple at Luxor was not enough of a monumental contribution, Amenhotep III also took on ambitious renovations at Karnak. There, Amenhotep III was responsible for the construction of a new pylon (pylon III). Located between Karnak's second and fourth pylons, the third pylon formed the eastern wall of the Great Hypostyle Hall, but in order to make room for the third pylon, Amenhotep III completely destroyed the festival court of Thutmose II, as well as the numerous pillars, bark shrines, and other monuments by which the festival court was decorated. Once dismantled, these elements were used in the foundation and fill of his new pylon.

Amenhotep III had his new pylon decorated predominately with reliefs glorifying his jubilee festival. The pylon's other reliefs depicted the pharaoh and the god's sacred bark on the festive journey to the temple at Luxor. Other scenes showed the king's son accompanying his father on this journey. On the southern processional route, Amenhotep III also began construction on Karnak's tenth pylon, but the king died before its construction was complete.

The most impressive of all the monuments built by Amenhotep III's was his mortuary temple, which was by far the largest mortuary temple on the west bank. The Colossi of Memnon, the stone statues of Amenhotep III which originally flanked the temple's entrance, were so impressive that they came to be known as one of the seven wonders of the ancient world.

A 19th century picture of the Colossi of Memnon

Chapter 3: The Amarna Period

Under the reign of the son and successor of Amenhotep III, Amenhotep IV (1353-1336 B.C.E.), Thebes was thrown into turmoil. Although Amenhotep III had left his son a peaceful and prosperous nation, Amenhotep IV was not content with the state of conditions in Thebes when he inherited from his father. In the first year of his reign, Amenhotep IV, like so many of his predecessors, took up work at Karnak, but instead of building a monument to Amun-Ra, Amenhotep IV built a new temple for the god Aten. The temple to Aten was fronted by an open court with a colonnade of square pillars, against which rested alternating colossal statues of Amenhotep IV and his queen Nefertiti.[14] The walls of the temple courtyard were decorated with painted reliefs which depicted the pharaoh and his queen entering and exiting the palace and making offerings to the gods during various parts of the royal jubilee festival. The complex of

---

[14] Though the eighteenth dynasty had seen some powerful women, the power Amenhotep IV bestowed upon Nefertiti was exceptional—her power was surpassed only by that of the pharaoh himself. Some scholars even suggest that Nefertiti ruled with Amenhotep IV as co-regent.

Amenhotep IV was enclosed by its own mud brick wall, and the structure was in no way connected to the preexisting temple complex.

A depiction of Akhenaten, Nefertiti, and their children

The famous bust of Nefertiti

This new temple complex built by Amenhotep IV served as a physical representation of the way in which the Amenhotep IV defied the regal precedent of his ancestors and departed from centuries of Theban traditions.

In the fifth or sixth year of his reign Amenhotep IV changed his name to Akhenaten and constructed a new capital city, Akhetaten (modern Amarna), far from the polluting influence of any other god who was not Aten. Akhetaten (Horizon of Aten) is located in middle Egypt in the al-Minya district, and it is known today as Amarna. The city was the capital of Ancient Egypt during the reign of Amenhotep IV, and it was custom built to be his administrative and religious capital.

After forming the identity of the god Aten, and Aten's new place in Egyptian theology as the "Grand Creator", Amenhotep IV strove to establish the new cult of the Aten in the traditional religious centers of Ancient Egypt, including that of Thebes. He even built a large temple complex to Aten in the main temple complex at Karnak, but he met with little success, as the cult of Amun-Ra was still too strong there. Thus, Amenhotep IV decided to take more drastic measures, including disbanding the priesthoods of all the gods except that of Aten and re-diverting the funds from those cults to that of Aten.

The city of Akhetaten was built very quickly, allowing for the royal court to establish residence there in year 5 of Amenhotep IV's reign. It was also around this time that he made the change from Amenhotep to Akhenaten, which roughly translates to "beneficial of the Aten" or "servant of the Aten".

Temple of the Aten in Akhetaten

While Akhetaten was undoubtedly the new religious center of Egypt, it is not clear what its administrative duties were. Memphis had long since been the administrative capital of Ancient Egypt, and while one of Akhenaten's viziers was stationed at Amarna, the other remained in Memphis, which implies that Memphis was still functioning as an administrative center. During the Saite Period, the reigns of the 26th dynasty kings offer a possible parallel. They set up their capital in the city of Sias, but Memphis remained an administrative center. Memphis did not lose its position as such until the advent of Alexander the Great, and his creation of the city of Alexandria, which soon became the religious, cultural, and political center of the country. So while administrative duties where probably seen to at Akhetaten, the administration of the whole of Egypt was still being overseen from Memphis.

That said, at some point, Akhenaten vowed never again to leave the boundaries of Akhetaten. In fact, a cache of letters recently discovered at the site suggests that Akhenaten's withdrawal from the outside world was so complete that under his rule Egypt no longer took any part in world affairs. In the 9th year of his reign, Akhenaten officially declared that Aten was the only god and that he was the sole intermediary between Aten and the Egyptian people. Akhenaten proscribed the worship of all other gods, including the traditional worship of Amun-Ra. Ordinary people, suddenly barred from the worship of their traditional gods, were not even permitted to worship Aten directly; instead, Akhenaten insisted that they worship him and the other members of the royal family as Aten's only earthly intermediaries. In essence, for the first time in Egyptian history, the pharaoh had absolute power over both secular and religious life in Egypt.[15]

Eventually, Akhenaten ordered Amun's name to cut from every temple in Egypt, going so far as to deface the name of his own father and forefathers because their names contained the name of Amun. Any inscription that made reference to a plurality of gods was also removed.

Akhenaten's reign is believed to have lasted from 1352-1336, and upon his death it is believed that he was buried not in the Valley of the Kings, which was the established burial area for the New Kingdom rulers, but in a royal tomb that was found outside of Akhetaten. Very little remains of the tomb, having suffered extensive damage in antiquity, but scattered remains of Akhenaten's sarcophagi indicate that he was most likely buried there.

The transition of power from Akhenaten to Tutankhamun is full of controversy. Before Tutankhamun, on the reignal lists, there are two other possible pharaohs, Smenkhare and Neferneferuaten. It is not known whether Smenkhare or Neferneferuaten ruled independently or if they were both co-regents with Akhenaten at some point. It has even been argued that they are one and the same person, though there is a general consensus that due to the feminine "t" ending found in Neferneferuaten's name that she was a female ruler. Smenkhare has a masculine name and is often depicted with another female by his side, presumably his wife, which makes it highly unlikely that the two rulers where the same person.

It is thought by some that Neferneferuaten was Nefertiti, although there is very little evidence to support this, short of Nefertiti having been known to use the title herself. While it is possible that Nefertiti ruled as co-regent with her husband, or even briefly on her own for a very short period after his death, there is no real evidence other than conjecture to support such a hypothesis.

Even less is known about Smenkhare, who may have been the younger brother of Akhenaten

---

[15] Power may have been a motivating factor in Akhenaten's conversion. Akhenaten's father, Amenhotep III, had been worried about the growing power of the priests of Amun. By establishing a new religious order which rejected Amun in favor of Aten (who could only be accessed through the royal family), Akhenaten would have wretched all power from the priests of Amun and restored it unto himself. The traditional temple-based economy would have also shifted to an economy run by government administrators and military commanders.

(though there is no evidence that proves such a familial connection). It is not known whether he ruled as co-regent before Neferneferuaten or after, or if he ruled independently for a time. The main documented reference to him as pharaoh comes from the tomb of Meryre II, in the Northern tomb necropolis at Amarna. Whilst the actual scene is lost, it is recorded that there was a scene depicting the king Smenkhare and his great wife Meritaten handing out tribute from a balcony or "window of appearance", just as Akhenaten and Nefertiti were so often depicted doing. With the scene now being lost it is difficult to determine Smenkhare's place within the royal 18th dynasty line. Very little is known about the end of Akhenaten's reign, and the possible rule of Smenkhare and/or Neferneferuaten. It is not until the reign of Tutankhamun that the historical record becomes clearer again.

Bjørn Christian Tørrissen's picture of the mask of Tutankhamun's mummy

Under the reign of the "heretic king" Akhenaten, Egypt had fallen into chaos, but as soon as his young son Tutankhaten took power, he began trying to repair some of the damage done by his father to the Egyptian empire. Almost immediately, Tutankhaten changed his name to Tutankhamun ("the living image of Amun" rather than "the living image of Aten"), ordered the royal court back to Thebes, and reversed his father's decree that had proscribed the worship of all gods except for Aten. It was Tutankhamun's hope that his restoration of the old order would cause the gods to once again look favorably upon Egypt and its empire.

Tutankhamun's Restoration Stela attests to these restoration attempts:

> "When his majesty appeared as king, the temples of the gods and goddesses from Elephantine to the marshes of the Delta [had... and] gone to pieces. Their shrines had become desolate, had become mounds overgrown with [weeds]. Their sanctuaries were as if they had never been. Their halls were a footpath (or trodden roads). The land was topsy-turvy and the gods turned their backs upon this land.
>
> His majesty made monuments for the gods by making their holy statues of genuine electrum of the best of the foreign lands. He recreated their sanctuaries as monuments until the limits of eternity, exquisitely equipped with offerings for all eternity, by endowing them with divine offerings as regular daily sacrifices and endowing them with provisions on earth. He gave more than had been formerly. He surpassed what had been done since the times of his ancestors. He introduce wab-priests and prophets of the children of the officials of their city, as the son of a man of note whose name was known. He multiplied their altars of gold, silver, bronze and copper and there was no end to all things. He filled their workhouses with male and female slaves from the supply of booty of his majesty. He increased all the taxes to the temples, doubling, trebling and quadrupling the silver, gold, lapis-lazuli, turquoise and all kinds of precious stones, royal linen, white linen, coloured linen, utensils, resin, fat, ... incense, frankincense, myrrh, without there being a limit to all the good things."

It is the nature of inscriptions detailing the pharaohs' regal deeds to be self-aggrandizing and often embellished, but there is unquestionably a lot of truth regarding the claims made in Tutankhamun's restoration stela. Furthermore, Tutankhamun's restoration attempts included some renewed building at Karnak. To the south of the temple precinct, along the processional route to the Mut temple, Tutankhamun added two lines of ram-headed[16] sphinx statues. Additionally, Tutankhamun built enclosing walls down either side of Amenhotep III's temple at Luxor. He also embellished the walls with reliefs showing scenes from the annual Opet festival (when Amun came to Luxor from Karnak to visit his southern harem).[17]

Tutankhamun died when he was only 18, and since the pharaoh had not been able to produce

---

[16] The ram, a symbol of fertility, came to be closely associated with Amun. In later periods, the ram came to replace the goose as Amun's sacred animal.

[17] Borne on the shoulders of white robed priests, sacred barges carried the sacred bark from Karnak to Luxor in a splendid procession. The Opet festival took place at the height of the Nile flooding and consisted of twenty four days of merrymaking and festivities.

an heir (his children were stillborn), he was succeeded by his great uncle and grandfather-in-law, Ay, who had been Tutankhamun's Grand Vizier and one of his closest advisors. Ay's reign was extremely short (he ruled for no more than seven years), and the historical record is largely silent as to what he accomplished during his brief tenure as pharaoh.

Part of Ay's absence in the historical record is due to his successor, Horemheb (1306-1292), who implemented a campaign of *damnatio memoriae*[18] against him and the other pharaohs who were associated with the unpopular Amarna Period. Horemheb did his best to destroy all monuments of Akhenaten, and he even used the remains of these monuments in his own building projects. At Karnak, Horemheb constructed a new pylon (pylon II), which significantly extended the temple to the west. The western face of the second pylon featured a large gateway, which would have served as the main gate to the temple. At the time of its construction, the second pylon fronted an open court that led to the third pylon of Amenhotep III. Horemheb decorated his pylons with scenes of himself in the company of the gods.

A picture of pylon II

Horemheb also built another pylon (pylon IX) between pylons VIII and X in order to further elaborate the southern processional route, and he utilized the *talatat* blocks from Akhenaten's temples in eastern Karnak as building fill. Horemheb also finished the construction of the tenth pylon of Amenhotep III and added sandstone walls (also filled with the rubble of Akhenaten's

---

[18] The Ancient Egyptians attached so much importance to the preservation of a person's name that the destruction of a person's name believed in some way to destroy the person himself, even if that person was no longer alive. Horemheb was so successful in wiping out the cartouches (a hieroglyphic symbol indicating a royal name) of his predecessors that they were forgotten by history for almost two millennia.

temples) in order to connect the ninth and tenth pylons. Once completed, the pylon featured a court which functioned as an intermediary space between the sacred and the profane. To the east of this court was a doorway leading to the temple's administrative quarters, storehouses, and the homes of the temple's priests. The towers of the tenth pylon depict Horemheb "smiting" his enemies, while the walls of the pylon's court are decorated with reliefs showing Horemheb on his journey to the legendary land of Punt and the fabulous treasures with which he returned. Horemheb left no direct successor—when he died, the eighteen dynasty died with him.

A picture of the ruins of pylon IX

Chapter 4: The New Kingdom Period

Horemheb was succeeded by his Grand Vizier, Ramses I, who became the founder of Egypt's 19th dynasty. Ramses traced his origins to northern Egypt, most likely to the eastern Delta, and it was to the eastern Delta that he moved the royal court. Nevertheless, the pharaohs of the 19th dynasty recognized the importance of Amun's cult at Thebes and continued to lavish it with wealth and attention. The early pharaohs of the 19th dynasty even made sure to spend part of every year residing at Thebes.

Like his predecessor, it was the main priority of Ramses I to reestablish order in the empire and reassert Egypt's power over Canaan and Syria. Accordingly, the pharaoh never found any time in his brief reign to construct any significant monuments.[19] Even his tomb was small and hastily finished.

Under Seti I (reigned 1290-1279), the son and successor of Ramses I, Egypt finally regained its former prosperity, and Thebes prospered in turn. Indeed, the restoration of Egypt's fortune was marked by a renaissance in building at Thebes. At Karnak, Seti I oversaw the construction of a new hypostyle hall, a huge multi-columned structure located between the second and third pylons. Filling the hall were 134 gigantic stone columns, while 12 open papyrus columns lined the raised central aisle. 122 clothed-bud papyrus-form columns stood north and south of the central aisle, and the first row of these columns on either side of the aisle supported the hall's stone ceiling and clerestory windows.

---

[19] A minor exception is the small station of the king which Ramses had added at Karnak. This station featured a calcite floor which was inscribed with the "nine bows," the traditional enemies of Egypt.

The hypostyle hall built under Seti I

Seti I decorated the northern half of the eastern interior wall with reliefs showing "the daily ritual." These reliefs highlighted the king's responsibility for maintaining the statue of Amun-Ra which was housed in Karnak's temple. In conjunction with that, the southern half of the west interior wall showed scenes of the temple foundation ceremony and featured images of the king and the gods performing the important rituals which needed to take place before a new building at the temple could be constructed.

Seti I also decorated the northern exterior side of the new hypostyle wall, as the exterior reliefs depict the king at battle with the enemies of Egypt. Its individual scenes showed Seti I's campaigns against the Shasu Bedouin, the Libyans, the Hittites, and the Yenoam Asiatics, as well as the submission and presentation of foreign rulers before the pharaoh, and the victorious king in turn presenting the spoils of war to the important Theban deities.

As the work made clear, the new hypostyle hall was the 19th dynasty's answer to the 18th dynasty's Wadjet Hall. This new hall provided an even more extravagant setting for festival processions and other festive occasions, and on some of these occasions, some of the Theban population was even allowed to enter the hall in order to view the king or the divine image in its portable bark.

An image of Seti I

Seti I died before he could finish decorating his hypostyle hall, but his son and successor, Ramses II (1279-1213), was eager to take on the task of completing his father's hall. It was left to Ramses the Great to decorate the hall's columns and its southern exterior wall, so he inscribed the larger columns with his own cartouches and the smaller southern columns with ritual scenes and a series of plant and bird motifs. Each of these smaller columns was also carved with a line of Ramses II's cartouches. Ramses II even ordered the preexisting cartouches of the clerestory window grills re-cut so that they bore his own name rather than the name of Seti I.

On the hall's southern exterior wall, Ramses II initially commissioned monumental sunken reliefs which glorified his military "triumph" against the Assyrians at the battle of Quadesh.[20] However, he ordered his artists to carve over these reliefs before they were completed. Quadesh had actually been a disaster for the Egyptians, even though Ramses successfully used propaganda to cast it as a victory, but eventually, the Quadesh reliefs were replaced with depictions of the military campaigns Ramses II had led in Syro-Palestine. These campaigns were carried out over 15 years, and the reliefs they inspired spilled onto the west wall of the court of the seventh pylon. These reliefs mirror the battle reliefs that his father, Seti I, had inscribed on the hall's northern exterior wall.

Ramses II was a prolific monument builder. In addition to finishing his father's hypostyle hall, Ramses II also constructed his own temple at Karnak. The temple of Ramses II (called "Amun-Ra, Ramses II who hears prayers") was located at the far eastern side of the temple complex, and it was built around the Obelisk Unique. The new temple consisted of a small mud-brick gateway that led into a pillared hall with a central false door. Two (real) doors then led out to a covered portico at the base of the obelisk.

The temple reused the column drums of Thutmose III, which suggests that Ramses II may have built a Thutmosid shrine in a nearby location. Furthermore, this temple seems to have functioned similarly to the contra temple built by Thutmose III, meaning it likely provided an entrance through which average Egyptians could enter the temple and pray to Amun Ra. Elsewhere in the eastern part of the temple complex, Ramses II raised a sphinx and a pair of rose granite obelisks.

At the temple of Luxor, Ramses II added an outer court, which featured a new double colonnade with colossal statues of Ramses II standing between its 74 papyrus columns. Colossal statues of the pharaoh also stood before the towers of his lofty new pylon at Luxor, and the walls of this pylon were decorated with sunken reliefs depicting Ramses II at war in Syria. On the façade of the western tower, the pharaoh could be seen interacting with his advisers and generals. The façade of the eastern tower showed Ramses II driving his chariot over his dead and dying enemies.

Ramses II was succeeded by his 13th son, Mernepath (reigned 1213-1203), who was too preoccupied with military campaigns to leave behind any kind of a monument, and ultimately, the prosperity of the 19th dynasty was relatively short lived. Their success peaked during the reigns of Seti I and Ramses II, but the reign of Mernepath's son and successor, Seti II (1200-1194), marked the beginning of a period of dynastic intrigue and short reigns. Seti II himself

---

[20] Most Egyptologists agree that this battle was actually a draw (at best).

only ruled for about six years, but at some point during his brief reign, Seti II found time to build a small triple shrine (called "the place of honoring and praying to all the gods") at Karnak. This shrine was located along the east-west processional route at a point outside of the temple's western entrance. Its southern face was covered with reliefs of Seti II making offerings to the Theban gods, but the blocks composing its northeast corner and west wall were left undressed. The shrine would have housed the barks of Mut (in the west), Khonsu (in the east) and Amun (in the center) during the various processions of the temple that were made by the statues of the gods. Since it existed outside of the temple's sacred space, the shrine of Seti II may have functioned as another place where average Egyptians could gather and pray.

A picture of the shrines of Seti II

As the prosperity of Thebes began to wane, the descendant of Seti II, Ramses III (1186-1155), became the last native Egyptian pharaoh to complete any significant New Kingdom monuments at Thebes. At the southwest corner of the temple precinct at Karnak, Ramses III constructed a temple to the god Khonsu.[21] A porch with open papyrus columns fronted the temple's main pylon, which led to an unroofed court that was enclosed by a double peristyle of closed-bud papyrus columns. There was also a small ramp in the court which led into the center of the

---

[21] Son of the god Amun-Ra and the goddess Mut

temple. The temple itself consisted of a small suite of rooms in which the statue of the god was housed, as well as a separate bark chamber.

South of the second pylon, Ramses also erected a new bark shrine. This shrine was fronted by its own small pylon, which featured a granite gateway and inscribed reliefs depicting scenes of the king smiting his enemies. 16 engaged statues of Ramses III adorned the pillars of the temple's first court, which led to a small vestibule and a hypostyle hall. Within the temple's inner sanctuary, Ramses erected a triple bark shrine which housed the sacred barks of Amun, Mut, and Khonsu.

During the latter part of Ramses III's reign, the Egyptian economy began to slip into crisis. The throne evidently did not have enough money to pay the workmen at Deir el-Medina, and the workmen responded with a general strike, the first in recorded history. The growing dissent soon led to an attempt on the pharaoh's life. At least 40 people were implicated and tried for plotting to kill the pharaoh and incite a revolt outside of the royal palace. The plot to kill the pharaoh failed, but Ramses III died during the trial of the conspirators.

Ramses III was succeeded by his son Ramses IV (1155-1149), whose reign was short but still somewhat prosperous. Like so many of his forefathers, Ramses IV was interested in the construction of monuments, and he apparently sent forth large expeditions for the sole purpose of acquiring stone for statues, but the turmoil that had plagued his father's reign seems to have posed a lingering threat. Of the 8,368 men who set out on this mission, at least 2,000 were soldiers whose purpose seemed to have more to do with controlling the workmen than it did defending them. Nevertheless, the men returned with enough materials for Ramses IV to build a new gateway for the court of the third pylon at Karnak as an elaboration of the southern processional entrance to the temple. This gateway was decorated extensively with sunken reliefs which featured imagery tied to the Theban festivals. Ramses IV also began construction on an expansive mortuary temple, but he encountered difficulties with the delivery of the necessary commodities and abandoned the project in favor of a smaller, less demanding structure.

Chapter 5: The Intermediate Period and Late Period

In the mid-12th century, the 20th dynasty was once again shaken by controversy. After an accusation posed by the mayor of the east bank of the Nile at Thebes against his colleague on the west bank, the royal court, by the order of Ramses IV, began to investigate the plundering of royal tombs in the Valley of the Kings. These investigations found that the royal mummies had been plundered and moved from place to place until the priests of Amun finally deposited them in a tomb shaft at Dayr al-Bahri and in the tomb of Amenhotep II.[22]

This egregious corruption left Thebes in a state of unrest, and as power began to pass

---

[22] It seems as though this move had more to do with "recycling" the wealth of the grave goods than it did with ensuring their security.

increasingly from the pharaohs to the high priests of Amun, Egypt entered its Third Intermediate Period (1069-715). So great was the power acquired by these priests that when the last Ramses (Ramses V) died of smallpox in 1145, the government of Egypt came to be shared between the royal dynasty at Tanis and the high pontiff at Thebes. Some priests even went so far as to write their names in cartouches.

The 21st dynasty did not vie with the priests for total control of the state; instead, they allied themselves with the priests by using intermarriage and adoption to forge strong ties with their co-dynasts. Installing their daughters as the "god's wife of Amun" (the highest ranking priestess of the Amun cult) at Thebes also allowed the pharaohs of the 21st dynasty to wield some power there. It was during the 21st dynasty that a monument was officially commissioned by a priest instead of a pharaoh, a first in Theban history. In 1054, the high priest Pindejem began the construction of some 100 sphinxes along the western processional way.

By the middle of the 10th century, the 21st dynasty had already reached its end, and the 22nd dynasty was far less content to let the priests continue their rule at Thebes. Sheshonq I (943-922), the first pharaoh of this dynasty, installed his son Iuput as the Governor of Upper Egypt, High Priest of Amun, and commander-in-chief of all his armies, a move which united the empire's religious and secular elements and allowed Sheshonq I to exert control over the problematic Theban region. Sheshonq I also installed his son, Djedptahaufankh, as the Third Prophet of Amun so that he could offer support to his brother. He installed yet another son, Nimlot, as military commander at Herakleopolis. The military base at Herakleopolis was located close enough to Thebes to allow its soldiers to keep the region in check.

Sheshonq I was the first pharaoh in nearly two centuries to undertake any new construction at Karnak. Sheshonq built the temple's first court, which he placed between the first and second pylons, and this court enclosed the Seti II shrine and the northern section of the Ramses III temple. Sandstone papyrus bud columns lined the courts northern and southern sides. The court likely contained a magnificent new gateway, as a stela from the 21st year of Sheshonq I's reign claims that he intended to "illuminate Thebes by erecting its double door of millions of cubits, to make a festival court for the house of his father Amun-Ra, king of the gods."

Between the Temple of Ramses III and the second pylon, Sheshonq I also built a structure now known as the "Bubasite Portal" (after Bubastis, the pharaoh's home city). Inside the court, the Bubasite Portal was marked by two closed papyrus columns, one on either side. Sheshonq had the exterior face of his portal decorated with a series of relief scenes which commemorated his great military victories in Syro-Palestine. Many scenes depicted the pharaoh smiting his enemies while the god Amun and the goddess Mut hold the cords that bind the hands and throats of the captives. Other parts of the wall were decorated with 156 "name rings" (symbols of bound captives with the names of ancient cities or tribes inside) and various inscriptions cataloging the towns and peoples Sheshonq I claimed to have defeated.

The Bubasite Portal with a depiction of Sheshonq I and Iuput

Shortly after the death of Sheshonq I, Egypt was once again consumed by turmoil and civil war, and Karnak would see no new construction for over three centuries. As this suggests, the 22nd dynasty did not enjoy their power for long, and within a century of their ascent, a rival 23rd dynasty had arisen at Leontopolis in the central Delta. At first, the Thebans allied themselves with the new rulers, but when Nubia became a contender in the Egyptian power struggle in the middle of the 8th century, the situation changed rapidly. The Nubian pharaohs of the 25th[23] dynasty originally ruled from Napata, but they quickly began to extend their power and influence northward until one Nubian pharaoh, Piankhy (752-721), took control of Thebes around 740. Piankhy was succeeded by his brother, Shabaka (721-707), who quickly defeated his Delta rivals and united the Egyptian nation once again.

The pharaohs of the 25th dynasty were foreigners, and as such, they preferred to be buried near their Nubian capital. However, in all other respects, the new rulers were quick to adopt Egyptian customs, and their tombs were the first regal pyramids to be constructed in nearly a millennium.

The Nubian pharaoh Taharqua (690-664), still anxious to convince native Egyptians to accept their new regime, undertook a number of projects - both restorations and expansions - at Karnak. On the northern side of the sacred lake, Taharqua constructed a rectangular cult building using blocks that had been inscribed for his predecessor. Its sandstone edifice consisted of a series of subterranean passages, as well as a superstructure with a central open court. A deep stone well (the "Nilometer") cut through the center of the courtyard.

The exterior northern and southern walls of the edifice were decorated with sunken reliefs which depicted the king and various gods. The first scene of these reliefs showed the king as he left his palace, while ensuing scenes showed him as he greeted the gods and made the sacrifices necessary to enter the temple. Reliefs on the interior walls featured the litanies of the sun, as well as some scenes associated with the decade festival. The structure was used for rituals concerning Amun-Ra's return from the west bank, the god's union with Nun, and the creative powers of the primeval waters. Furthermore, it housed the celebration of the union of the gods Osiris and Amun.

In the temple's first court, Taharqo installed an impressive limestone kiosk which consisted of two rows of five large open papyrus form columns. These were connected with low screen walls to form the free-standing edifice, though the huge distance between the two aisles suggests that the structure was unroofed. The entire area was paved with rose granite stones, and a calcite shrine in the center of the kiosk supported the bark of the god, while doorways within the screen walls opened to all four sides of the court. The kiosk is believed to have functioned in the "union of the disc" ceremony, in which the cult statue of Amun-Ra was brought out from his *naos* to unite with the solar disk so that he could be re-energized.

Once again, this burst of construction at Karnak would be followed by several centuries of almost no building activity. In 671, during the middle of Taharqo's reign, Assyrian invaders arrived in Egypt. One of these Assyrians, Esarhaddon, invaded and captured Memphis, forcing Taharqo to flee south to Thebes, but in 664, Esarhaddon's son Ashurbanipal invaded and sacked

---

[23] There was, of course, a twenty fourth dynasty, but it seems to have been historically insignificant. It saw only two rulers, and the sum total of their rule was roughly twelve years.

Thebes as well. The city's great temple complexes at Luxor and Karnak, which had stood for nearly two millennia, were looted and laid to waste, and the defeated Nubian pharaohs retreated to their homeland.

Ashurbanipal left Egypt under the control of the Saite pharaohs of the 26th dynasty, and the new rulers left Thebes to its own devices. The pharaohs of this dynasty gave control of the city to mayors who held religious authority, as they had been vested with the Divine Adoratices of Amun. As long as these mayors paid tribute on time, the Assyrians were not concerned with local Egyptian affairs.

An ancient Assyrian depiction of Ashurbanipal as a high priest

Ashurbanipal died in 627, and the Assyrian Empire began to fall into a swift decline. Given this power vacuum, the provinces of Egypt were filled with dynastic disputes and widespread discontent, both of which left it weak and vulnerable to attacks from the outside by the Medes and Persians in Iran, as well as the Scythians and Cimmerians in Central Asia.

Left to their own devices by the preoccupied Assyrians, the 26th dynasty was able to extend their authority upstream, but the Assyrian empire was replaced by the Babylonian Empire. Then came the empire of the Medes, and then the Persian Empire. With the use of Greek and Anatolian mercenaries, the Egyptian pharaohs were able to remain largely independent, but the rulers of these great empires dealt with pharaohs who grew too ambitious quickly and harshly. The pharaoh Necho (610-595) dreamed of restoring the Egyptian empire to the greatness it had seen under Ramses and Thutmose, but his dreams and his army were quickly destroyed by the Babylonian king Nebuchadnezzar at the Battle of Carchemish in 605.

In 525, the Persian king Cambyses arrived in Egypt to destroy Psamtik III, the last pharaoh of the 26th dynasty, at Pelusium. Though Psamtik III fled to Memphis, he was soon captured there and sent to Susa, the Persian capital, to be executed. Henceforth, the Persians administered Egypt as a satrapy, so the governors of the satrapy became, in a sense, the pharaohs of Egypt's 27th dynasty.

By the end of the 5th century, native Egyptian rulers had begun to reassert themselves, and by the beginning of the 4th century, this renewed Egyptian rule was marked by a renewal of building activity at Thebes, the first in nearly three centuries. Ground was broken once again in Karnak in 393 by the Egyptian pharaoh Psammuthis, who ordered the construction of a mud brick storehouse and an aviary on the south side of Karnak's sacred lake. The storehouse, which was raised above the lake on a platform, could be accessed with stairs on both its eastern and western sides, and it featured a central open air court which was lined on its southern edges by a portico of eight columns. A canal leading from the court to the Sacred Lake allowed the sacred geese to enter and exit the magazine at will. In the northeast corner of the structure was another small court which was set aside for animal slaughter. The storehouse's hallways led to small storage rooms and small shrines. The shrines were home to a number of sandstone *naoi*, and inscriptions on this structure indicate that it functioned as a shena-wab, a place for the preparation of the god's daily meals.

Psammuthis' successor, Hakor (391-380), also took an interest in building at Thebes. Hakor constructed a small rectangular chapel outside pylon I of the great temple to Amun-Ra. The chapel had two doorways, with one opening to the west and the other to the north. The western half of the chapel was composed of open papyrus form columns, while the chapel's eastern side was fully enclosed. A wooden architrave supported its stone cavetto blocks.

A picture of pylon I

Hakor's chapel was used to house the portable bark of Amun-Ra on its processional journey outside the temple. With this procession in mind, the design of the chapel was ingenious, as the bark could be moved directly from the river into the shrine (via the northern door) and then removed again (through the western door) without changing the orientation of the bark as it entered the temple precinct. A small platform was even placed in the chapel's rear so that Amun's priests could rest the bark upon it while they themselves changed positions.

Of the three Egyptian pharaohs who participated in the Late Period building renaissance at Thebes, Nectanebo I (379-361) was by far the most prolific builder. South of the Khonsu Temple, Nectanebo erected a sphinx-lined alleyway which led up to a magnificent gate. The ceilings of the gate were decorated with flying vultures, and its interior walls were covered with hieroglyphics which read "all life, prosperity, and health." Its northern face was decorated with relief scenes showing the pharaoh interacting with Egypt's divinities. The center of the gate's lintel was adorned with a winged sun-disk.

Nectanebo also commissioned a temple to Opet, the hippopotamus goddess. The Opet Temple was located in the southwest of the Amun precinct, just west of the Khonsu temple. Direct access to the Opet Temple was provided by a gateway on the southwest side of the temple enclosure wall. A small pylon and a columned porch stood before the western side of the temple; within its court was a columned kiosk. From the court, a ramp provided access to the temple's small hypostyle hall, which boasted two Hathor-headed columns. The hall led to the temple's main sanctuary, which featured a niche for the divinity statue. A series of crypts ran down from the temple into its platform. One claimed to be the tomb of Osiris, and another served as a "birth chamber." A small shrine for the cult statue of Osiris was erected at the temple's rear-exterior wall and could be accessed from the outside.

Most ambitiously, Nectanebo I began to construct yet another new pylon to serve as a new monumental entrance to the temple and perhaps to protect the temple from the threat of foreign invaders. Ironically, however, the Babylonians invaded in 342 in order to (re)subjugate an area they still considered part of their empire. The first pylon was never completed, and the remains of the mud brick ramps used in its initial construction can still be seen at Karnak today.

Chapter 6: The Ptolemies and Beyond

The new Persian regime was so brutal that Alexander the Great's arrival in Egypt in 332 seems to have been met with relief by native Egyptians.[24] Though Alexander was acclaimed as a pharaoh, he did not remain in Egypt for long, and it is unlikely that he even visited Thebes.

---

[24] A shrine to Alexander the Great was erected in one of the halls of the temple at Luxor.

A bust of Alexander the Great

Upon his death in 323, rule of his empire passed first to his brother Philip (323-317) and then to his son, Alexander IV (317-305). However, by the end of the 4th century, Alexander's once vast empire had already been divided among his generals, and Ptolemy I took control of Egypt, thereby founding the 32nd and final dynasty of Ancient Egypt.

A bust of Ptolemy I

Ptolemy I took the new city Alexandria as his capital, and it was upon Alexandria rather than Thebes that he and his descendants would lavish their attentions.[25] The Ptolemies continued to

---

[25] One notable exception to this statement is Ptolemy IV, who completed the last known significant building project at Thebes. Near the end of the third century, Ptolemy IV began to construct the "Osiris catacombs" at the northeast corner of the great temple to Amun-Ra in Karnak. The structure was made of baked mud bricks; it consisted of a short hallway that provided access to three different galleries. A series of small niches lined these galleries—each niche was originally closed off with a clay plaque. The brick walls of the catacombs were plastered over and painted with the name of Ptolemy IV, as well as images of the resurrection of Osiris, and the running of the Apis bull. The catacombs were, of course, partly subterranean, and they were dedicated to Osiris,

rule Egypt from Alexandria until August 12, 30 BCE, when the infamous queen Cleopatra committed suicide after Marc Antony's forces were defeated by Octavian (later Augustus) at the naval battle of Actium. Henceforth, Egypt was absorbed into the Roman Empire, whose armies occasionally made camps at Thebes and painted murals in the Luxor Temple.

The emperor Constantine converted to Christianity and ultimately converted the Roman Empire along with him during the early 4th century CE, and about 80 years later, the Roman emperor Theodosius forbade the worship of the old gods and ordered all pagan temples, including the temple complexes at Karnak and Luxor, closed. The neglected sites rapidly fell into decay, and those that were not quarried for their stone were covered by the drifting sands, where they would remain, forgotten to the world, for almost two millennia.

Online Resources

Other books about Ancient Egypt by Charles River Editors

Other books about Ancient Egypt on Amazon

Other books about Ancient Thebes on Amazon

Bibliography

Dorman, Peter F. "Thebes." *Encyclopedia Britannica*. 9 June 2015. Web. 29 June 2015.

Drower, Margaret S. "Karnak." *Encyclopedia Britannica*. Web. 29 June 2015.

Drower, Margaret S. "Luxor." *Encyclopedia Britannica*. Web. 29 June 2015.

Drower, Margaret S. "Valley of the Kings." *Encyclopedia Britannica*. Web. 29 June 2015.

Dunn, Jimmy. "Ramses III: Egypt's Last Great Pharaoh." *Tour Egypt*. Web. 29 June 2015.

Gibson, Gail. "Amun." *Odyssey: Adventures in Archaeology*. 20 Nov. 2011. Web. 29 June 2015.

Gibson, Gail. "Deir el-Bahri: Temple of Mentuhotep." *Odyssey: Adventures in Archaeology*. Web. 29 June 2015.

Gibson, Gail. "Egyptian Temples." *Odyssey: Adventures in Archaeology*. 19 Aug. 2010. Web. 29 June 2015.

Gibson, Gail. "Thebes." *Odyssey: Adventures in Archaeology*. 22 Nov. 2011. Web. 29 June

---

the god of the underworld. The building functioned as a *hypogeum* (underground burial place). While most *hypogea* were used for the burials of sacred animals, the *hypogea* at Karnak were used for the burials of small statuettes of Osiris.

2015.

Hefner, Alan G, ed. "Amun." *Mythical-Folk*. 13 April 2013. Web. 29 June 2015.

Hill, J. "Akhenaten (Amenhotep IV)." *Ancient Egypt Online*. 2010. Web. 29 June 2015.

Murnane, William J. "The Bark of Amun on the Third Pylon at Karnak." *Journal of the American Research Center in Egypt*. Vol. 16 (1979), pp. 11-27.

University of California at Los Angeles. *Digital Karnak*. Ed. Ewan Branda. 2008. Web. 29 June 2015.